FACTS!

One for every day of the year

written by
TRACEY TURNER

illustrated by
FATTI BURKE

BLOOMSBURY
LONDON OXFORD NEW YORK NEW DELHI SYDNEY

Bloomsbury Children's Books
An imprint of Bloomsbury Publishing Plc

50 Bedford Square
London
WC1B 3DP
UK

1385 Broadway
New York
NY 10018
USA

www.bloomsbury.com

A catalogue record for this book is available from the British Library.

Library of Congress Cataloguing-in-Publication data has been applied for.

ISBN
HB: 9781408884621

2 4 6 8 10 9 7 5 3 1

Printed and bound in China by Leo Paper Products, Heshan, Guangdong

To find out more about our authors and books visit www.bloomsbury.com.
Here you will find extracts, author interviews, details of forthcoming
events and the option to sign up for our newsletters.

The facts in this book have come from a huge number of sources. Below
are just a few of the best. Take a look to find more fascinating facts:

Bbc.co.uk/learning

Britishmuseum.org

Dkfindout.com

Nasa.gov

Nationalgeographic.com

Nhm.ac.uk (Natural
History Museum)

Oceanmammalinst.org

Oum.ox.ac.uk (Oxford
University Museum of
Natural History)

Sciencemuseum.org.uk

Si.edu/museums
(Smithsonian Institution)

Wellcomecollection.org

INTRODUCTION

No one should ever be without a fascinating fact at their fingertips, and this book provides you with one for every single day of the year! Some of the facts are about things that happened on a particular date, or special holidays or feast days, but most are completely random, and totally astonishing.

Find out . . .
- Which animal does cube-shaped poos
- Some ancient cures for toothache
- How aliens from Mars terrified the people of America
- Which fish sleeps in a cosy layer of its own slime

Read on to discover the mysteries of the universe, farting herrings, Viking gods, and hundreds more amazing facts.

Some of the facts in this book happened on specific dates: look out for them in circles like this.

1 JANUARY
NEW YEAR'S DAY

In Scotland and northern England, the first person to cross your threshold on New Year's Day is very important. Superstitious people believe that a woman or a fair-haired man is bad luck, but a dark-haired man is also bad luck, if he's got flat feet!

2 JANUARY

When you sneeze, millions of tiny, germ-laden snot particles come whizzing out of your nose at about 65 kilometres per hour, and can spread for about one metre. Next time you see someone about to sneeze remember to dive for cover!

3 JANUARY

The Sargasso Sea is the only sea in the world that doesn't have a shore. It's an area of the Atlantic Ocean, over 1,000 kilometres wide and 3,200 kilometres long, bounded by ocean currents. It's famous for a type of seaweed called Sargassum, and eels that hatch and later travel thousands of kilometres back there to lay their eggs.

4 JANUARY

Is it a meteor or a meteorite?

A meteor is a lump of rock flying through space that burns up in the Earth's atmosphere. Also known as shooting stars, we see them as streaks of light in the night sky. A meteorite is also a lump of space rock, but one that doesn't completely burn up: it flies through our atmosphere and makes it all the way to Earth. Most meteorites are bits of asteroid from the asteroid belt between Jupiter and Mars. Some even make craters when they hit the Earth's surface.

5 JANUARY

Tiger sharks are some of the least fussy fish in the sea. They'll eat anything (including people). Dead tiger sharks have been found with all kinds of things in their stomachs, including a chicken coop, a car number plate, deer antlers, and medieval armour.

6 JANUARY

According to a Greek legend, underground goblins called Kallikantzaroi are intent on causing havoc between 25th December and 6th January. Legend says that to avoid them you must leave an empty colander on your doorstep, or burn old shoes... stinky!

7 JANUARY

Did you know that not all blood is red? Lots of creatures have yellow or green blood, including the yellow-footed, green-blooded skink (a type of lizard), and cockroaches, which have white blood!

8 JANUARY

Martin Strel, a long-distance swimmer from Slovenia, became the first person to swim the entire length of the River Amazon, in 2007 – all 5,268 kilometres of it . The river is home to all sorts of dangerous animals, including sharp-toothed piranha fish, crocodile-like caimans, huge and deadly anaconda snakes, and electric eels.

9 JANUARY

The Spruce Goose is the biggest plane ever built. It's more than 65 metres long, and its wingspan is nearly 100 metres! It only ever flew once, in 1947. It was built to carry soldiers and weapons during the Second World War, but by the time it was ready to fly the war was already over. Today it's on display at the Evergreen Aviation and Space Museum in Oregon, USA.

10 JANUARY

In the first days of the London Underground, people were worried about the safety of the escalators. A one-legged man called Bumper Harris was employed to use the escalators all day long to prove to people that they were safe, even if you only had one leg!

11 JANUARY

Human beings are one of 1.3 million recorded species of living things on planet Earth. New species are being discovered at the rate of around 15,000 every year! No one knows how many weird and wonderful life forms are still waiting to be discovered.

12 JANUARY

Find out about five of the world's slimiest animals . . .

1 HAGFISH
The eel-like hagfish is the slimiest animal in the world. It feeds on dead sea creatures, and oozes thick slime when attacked.

2 OPOSSUM
Cute-looking, but don't be fooled: it produces green, foul-smelling slime from its rear end when threatened.

VIOLET SEA SNAIL

This snail has a weird way of getting about: it floats on a raft of its own slime.

PARROTFISH

This colourful fish covers itself in a thick layer of slime to sleep in. Cosy!

VELVET WORM

Watch out: this worm can shoot two sticky ropes of slime, up to 30 centimetres long, to tie up its prey.

13 JANUARY

A 2,500-year-old graveyard has been discovered in Israel. People weren't buried in it though – instead, it was the final resting place for hundreds of dogs. Each of the 700 or so dogs was carefully buried in exactly the same position.

14 JANUARY

Emperor penguins are the biggest penguin species, and can measure up to 1.2 metres tall. In the snowy wastes of Antarctica, they hatch their young in temperatures colder than any other bird: –40°C, with a freezing wind of up to 144 kilometres per hour. The male penguins huddle together for warmth all winter long, protecting their chicks underneath their bodies, while they wait for the female penguins to return from fishing.

15 JANUARY

Kyle MacDonald wanted a house but didn't have much money. So in 2006 he decided to try swapping things to make his dream come true. He started off with a paper clip, and a few swaps later he had a van. Fourteen swaps after he started, he had a house! Swaps included a novelty doorknob, a snowmobile, and an afternoon with rock star Alice Cooper.

16 JANUARY

About a million earthquakes happen every year, but most of them are so weak people might not even notice them. Hang on, what was that? Someone's stomach rumbling – or an earthquake?

17 JANUARY
ON THIS DATE

Benjamin Franklin was born on 17th January 1706. He's best known for being one of the founding fathers of the United States and drawing up the Declaration of Independence. But he was busy with lots of other things too: he experimented with electricity, invented bifocal spectacles and a musical instrument called a glass armonica, and organised the first lending library in the United States.

18 JANUARY

Napoleon Bonaparte's wife, Josephine, had a pet orangutan. She would sometimes invite it to her dinner parties.

19 JANUARY

Tsunamis are huge waves, usually started by an earthquake on the sea bed, which build in power as they cross the ocean and come crashing into land, with disastrous results. A tsunami in the Indian Ocean in 2004 was the most deadly ever recorded – around 250,000 people lost their lives.

20 JANUARY

Rabbits, guinea pigs and baby elephants all eat their own poo.

21 JANUARY

Ancient Greek doctor Hippocrates, known as the father of modern medicine, thought it was a good idea to smell and taste patients' snot, pee, and earwax. He was the first person to say that diseases weren't caused by evil spirits, a revolutionary opinion at the time.

22 JANUARY

The Sun is our closest star – it's 149,597,893 kilometres away from Earth. Light from the Sun takes eight minutes and 17 seconds to get to Earth.

23 JANUARY
THE SEVEN WONDERS OF THE ANCIENT WORLD

The list was made in the Middle Ages, based on lists made by ancient Greek writers about wonderful constructions.

THE STATUE OF ZEUS AT OLYMPIA

The statue was 12 metres tall and made from gold and ivory.

THE HANGING GARDENS OF BABYLON

They disappeared long ago, but the story goes that King Nebuchadnezza had the spectacular gardens made for his wife.

THE GREAT PYRAMID AT GIZA, EGYPT

The Great Pyramid is more than 4,500 years old. It's the only one of the Seven Wonders that you can still go and wonder at.

THE LIGHTHOUSE AT ALEXANDRIA

When it was built around 280 BC, the lighthouse was one of the world's tallest buildings at about 120 metres. It would be tiny compared to our skyscrapers – the tallest one today is the Burj Khalifa, which is 829.8 metres tall!

THE TEMPLE OF ARTEMIS AT EPHESUS

This ancient Greek marble temple is supposed to have taken 120 years to build. The Goths destroyed it in AD 262.

THE MAUSOLEUM AT HALICARNASSUS

The elaborate tomb of King Mausolus was built in the fourth century BC. It was so magnificent that it inspired the word 'mausoleum', which is used to describe a grand tomb.

THE COLOSSUS OF RHODES

This giant bronze statue of the sun god Helios straddled Rhodes harbour, before it was destroyed in an earthquake.

24 JANUARY
THE SEVEN WONDERS OF THE NATURAL WORLD

There's no official list,
but people often agree on:

THE GREAT BARRIER REEF

A beautiful, huge coral reef
off the coast of Australia, home
to thousands of sea creatures.

VICTORIA FALLS

Huge, impressive waterfalls
in Zambia and Zimbabwe.

MOUNT EVEREST

The world's tallest mountain,
in Nepal and Tibet.

THE GRAND CANYON

An immense canyon
carved out by the
Colorado River in
Arizona, USA.

12

THE NORTHERN LIGHTS

The phenomenon of beautiful coloured lights in northern night skies, caused by solar wind particles.

PARICUTIN VOLCANO

A volcano born in 1943 in Paricutin, Mexico. This was the first time that scientists were able to witness the complete life of a volcano, from birth to extinction.

THE HARBOUR OF RIO DE JANEIRO

A large, spectacular bay surrounded by mountains in Brazil.

25 JANUARY

Although steam power wasn't used to power machines until more than a thousand years later, an ancient Greek called Hero invented the steam engine around AD 50. No one saw its potential and forgot about it. It was another 1,650 years before Thomas Savery invented a steam pump, and steam went on to power the Industrial Revolution.

26 JANUARY

All the Great Apes – gorillas, orangutans and chimpanzees – are endangered species, mainly because the forests where they live are being cut down at an alarming rate.

27 JANUARY
ON THIS DATE

The German composer Wolfgang Amadeus Mozart was born on 27th January 1756. He wrote his first symphony when he was eight years old. Have you written yours yet?

28 JANUARY

The most expensive pizza ever sold cost £2,150 and was made to raise funds for a charity in 2007. Toppings included caviar, champagne, lobster, venison, brandy, and flakes of edible gold!

29 JANUARY

Cockroaches can live for up to a week without their heads. This is because they don't have blood pressure in the same way we do (so they don't bleed uncontrollably). They breathe through holes called spiracles (rather than their mouths), and they don't have a brain in the same way we do. They eventually die because they can't drink water or eat.

30 JANUARY

The planets in our solar system from nearest the Sun to furthest away:

- Mercury
- Venus
- Earth
- Mars
- Jupiter
- Saturn
- Uranus
- Neptune

Pluto used to be the ninth planet, but it was demoted in 2006 to a dwarf planet (poor Pluto!). There's a theory that there's another planet out there, beyond Pluto, orbiting the Sun very slowly.

31 JANUARY

Never shake hands with a bushbaby: the animals pee on their paws so that they leave a smelly trail wherever they go.

1 FEBRUARY

Not all maps are drawn on paper. The people of Greenland carved maps into pieces of wood 300 years ago. They used 3D maps to navigate the coastline by touching them instead of looking at them.

2 FEBRUARY

The Milky Way got its name because it looks like a band of milky light from Earth – in fact we're looking side-on at a galaxy (our own) of billions of stars. It was called 'the road of milk' in Latin, and 'the circle of milk' in ancient Greek. In Iceland and Norway it's called the Winter Way, and in Finland it's The Path of the Birds. In China, Japan, North and South Korea, Taiwan and Mongolia it's called the Silver River.

3 FEBRUARY

The world's biggest seed is a type of coconut called a coco de mer, which can weigh up to 20 kilogrammes – the average weight of a six-year-old child!

4 FEBRUARY

The world's biggest egg is an ostrich egg, which is around 15 centimetres long and around 1.4 kilogrammes. That's about the same weight as 24 chicken eggs!

5 FEBRUARY

Bacteria are the toughest living things on the planet. These single-celled organisms come in many different types. Some of them can live in permanently frozen ground, while others thrive in the extreme heat of hydrothermal vents (cracks in the sea bed where superheated water gushes out from the hot depths of the Earth).

6 FEBRUARY

The novelist Charlotte Brontë fell in love with her French teacher. She wrote him love letters, which he tore up and threw in the bin because he was already married. His wife found the ripped-up pieces and, in the days before sticky tape, she stitched them together with a needle and thread so she could read them. The letters still survive today.

7 FEBRUARY

The ancient civilisation in the Indus Valley is mysterious – it was only discovered 150 years ago, and no one knows much about it. Cities, such as Mohenjo-Daro, were built more than 4,000 years ago, with roads, sewers, and even toilets, but no huge palaces or temples. Its written language hasn't been deciphered yet. But we do know that the area was the birthplace of dentistry: drilled teeth were discovered there from around 9,000 years ago!

8 FEBRUARY

Did you know that Antarctica is a desert? That's because it hardly ever rains there – in fact, in the Dry Valleys of Antarctica, it hasn't rained for *millions* of years!

9 FEBRUARY

When Halley's comet appeared in 1910, people panicked because of rumours about dangerous gas in the tail of the comet. The rumours were nonsense, but 'anti-comet pills' and 'comet protecting umbrellas' were sold to gullible customers.

10 FEBRUARY

Flamingos pee down their legs as a way of cooling down.

11 FEBRUARY
ON THIS DATE

Inventor Thomas Edison was born on 11th February 1847. He recorded more than one thousand inventions in his lifetime, including the phonograph, a machine that recorded sound. His own voice was the first sound to be recorded on it, saying the words 'Mary had a little lamb'.

12 FEBRUARY

Five unusual phobias . . .

- Blennophobia: fear of slime.
- Bufonophobia: fear of toads.
- Ephibiphobia: fear of children and teenagers.
- Coulrophobia: fear of clowns.
- Omphalophobia: fear of bellybuttons.

13 FEBRUARY

The pelicans in St James's Park, London, have been known to swallow whole, live pigeons. Gruesome and greedy!

14 FEBRUARY
VALENTINE'S DAY

Saint Valentine was a martyr in Rome in the third century, who is now associated with love and marriage. In the 1800s, his remains were discovered in a tomb near Rome, and bits of his skeleton are on display all around Europe: in Ireland, Scotland, England, France and the Czech Republic.

15 FEBRUARY

The ancient Roman Emperor Hadrian (famous for his wall across the north of England) started a fashion for beards. It's said he grew one to hide his warty chin!

16 FEBRUARY

Sharks are excellent predators because of their amazing senses: two thirds of a shark's brain is dedicated to its sense of smell! They can detect tiny vibrations in the water, and they can feel other creatures' electrical fields. Lesson – never play hide and seek with a shark.

17 FEBRUARY

John Harrington, Queen Elizabeth I of England's godson, invented a new type of flushing toilet in the 1590s. The Queen didn't like the toilet, and she was so cross with Harrington for writing a rude book about it (which mentioned poo a lot) that she banished him from the royal court.

18 FEBRUARY

Humans are the only animals to have developed language, but a chimpanzee called Washoe was the first animal to be taught sign language. Other apes and monkeys have learned it too.

19 FEBRUARY

Thousands of years ago people worked out that the Earth is a sphere. An ancient Greek called Eratosthenes even worked out its circumference using sticks and the lengths of shadows at noon, and some complicated maths. He was pretty accurate!

20 FEBRUARY

Cattle contribute to global warming because they produce methane, a greenhouse gas, in their burps, farts and manure. Each cow produces more than 100 litres of methane every day, and there are more than 1.3 billion of them in the world. That's a lot of methane! Scientists are experimenting with different diets to reduce the amount of methane produced by cattle, including feeding them garlic.

21 FEBRUARY

Frogs and fish have absolutely no business falling from the sky, yet rainfalls of these and other creatures are reported every so often. Rains of fish are the most common, yet the cause remains a mystery. Here are five weird rainfalls:

There was a rain of worms in Louisiana, USA, in 2007. Some of the worms were still alive after they'd landed.

In Japan, there were rains of tadpoles and froglets, and one rain of small carp, during June 2009.

In the town of Yoro, Honduras, rainfalls of sardines are so regular that there's an annual festival to celebrate them.

22 FEBRUARY
ON THIS DATE

George Washington, the first president of the United States, was born on 22nd February 1732. Washington had had almost all his teeth removed by the time he became president. He had several false sets, including one made from hippopotamus ivory and another from human teeth. Some of these were his own, which had been removed, and some he'd bought from other people (this sounds gruesome, but it was quite common for rich people to buy other people's teeth in those days!).

In 2010, the town of Rakoczifalva in Hungary was pelted with a rainfall of frogs.

In the same year in Lajamanu, a remote desert town in Australia, hundreds of spangled perch fell from the sky.

23 FEBRUARY

The ancient Romans left large containers in the street to collect the pee of passers-by, which they used to clean laundry. The Romans also used pee as a mouthwash to whiten teeth – they thought Portuguese pee was the best kind, and had it imported! Think of that next time you're gargling a minty fresh mouthwash...

24 FEBRUARY

People who can't stop picking their noses are said to have 'rhinotillexomania'.

25 FEBRUARY

Joan of Arc was a teenage farm girl who believed she was called by God to lead the French army. She really did take command of the French army and fought against the English at the age of 17. However, she was captured and killed by the English when she was only 19.

26 FEBRUARY

Gentoo penguins are the fastest penguin species – they can zoom along underwater at speeds of up to 35 kilometres per hour. That's faster than an Olympic rowing team!

27 FEBRUARY

The composer John Cage wrote 4'33" for the piano. It's four minutes and thirty-three seconds of complete silence. See if you can play it!

28 FEBRUARY

On average, each person releases around two litres of gas from their body as burps and farts every day. Most people fart around 14 times a day (hopefully well away from everyone else).

29 FEBRUARY
LEAP DAY

The 29 February comes only once every four years, in a leap year. There's an old-fashioned tradition that women are allowed to ask men to marry them on this day (but obviously they can do that any time they like). If the man refuses, he has to buy the woman 12 pairs of gloves!

1 MARCH

Five unusual patron saints:

- Saint Isodore of Seville, patron saint of the Internet.
- Saint Drogo, patron saint of unattractive people.
- Saint Martin of Tours, patron saint of geese.
- Saint Friard, patron saint of people who are afraid of wasps.
- Saint Apollonia, patron saint of dentists.

2 MARCH

Duck-billed platypuses are so strange that when people outside Australia first saw them they thought someone had stitched different animals together as a joke (but not a very funny one).

3 MARCH
ON THIS DATE

Alexander Graham Bell was born on 3 March 1847. He's famous for inventing the telephone, but also invented an early metal detector. The story goes that when US President Garfield was shot in 1881, Bell used his metal detector to search for the bullet. But he didn't find it because the doctor told him to look in the wrong part of the president's body!

4 MARCH

No one has ever been killed by a meteorite – at least no one we know about. However, there have been a few injuries: one woman was sitting on her sofa in Alabama, USA, when a meteorite smashed through the roof and bruised her leg.

5 MARCH

The world's most venomous snake is the inland taipan, also known as the fierce snake. The poison delivered in a single bite is enough to kill 100 people, and one bite can kill an adult in under an hour. Luckily, the snake is extremely unlikely to bite anyone – it isn't aggressive, and usually makes its home far away from people, in the grasslands of central Australia. There isn't a single recorded human death from an inland taipan's bite.

6 MARCH

The ancient Romans loved having baths and built public baths all over the Roman Empire. But they didn't use soap. Instead, the ancient Romans cleaned themselves by oiling their bodies, then using a special scraper called a strigil to scrape off the oil. If you were a posh Roman you might get your slave to do the scraping for you... I don't fancy that job!

7 MARCH

Around 153,000 people die each day, but on average 353,000 babies are born every day!

8 MARCH

The City Montessori School in Lucknow, India, is the world's biggest school. It teaches more than 50,000 pupils, aged between five and seventeen. How does this compare to your school?

9 MARCH

Cash money isn't always made of metal or paper. These have all been used as money in the past:

Pepper – Europe

Stones – Pacific Islands (on Yap in Micronesia, stone money is still used)

Coils of red feathers – Pacific Islands

Bread – Iraq

Dogs' teeth – New Guinea

Iron nails – Scotland

Whales' teeth – Fiji

10 MARCH

Bird's nest soup, a famous Chinese dish, really is made from birds' nests. It's made from the nests of a type of swallow, which uses its own saliva to build the nest.

11 MARCH

The ancient Greek playwright Aeschylus died when an eagle dropped a tortoise on his head!

12 MARCH

Several different types of sloth live in South America. These long-clawed mammals spend most of their time hanging from tree branches, barely moving. This makes them a good home for moths, other insects, and moss and algae, which can make a sloth's fur appear green in colour. They climb down to the ground to do a poo only once a week!

13 MARCH

In the past, make-up could be dangerous. Eyeshadows, lipsticks and face powder could contain dangerous chemicals, and some women made their eyes sparkle with the poisonous deadly nightshade plant. Skin was sometimes whitened with powder containing lead because pale skin was considered to be a sign of beauty.

14 MARCH

Saint Simeon Stylites lived on top of a pillar in Syria, for 37 years during the 400s, so that he could live a peaceful life of prayer away from the world. He started a fashion for holy men on pillars, and for about a hundred years after his death they were quite common!

15 MARCH

The Harvard Brain Tissue Resource Centre stores the world's largest collection of brains. They have 6,500.

6493

6494

6497

6498

16 MARCH

It wasn't all that long ago that women didn't have the right to vote in elections. Women gained the same voting rights as men at different times in different countries:

New Zealand: 1893

Australia: 1903 (South Australia granted women the vote in 1894)

Finland: 1907 (when it was part of the Russian Empire)

Norway: 1913

Russia: 1917

United States: 1920

Ireland: 1922

United Kingdom: 1928

Spain: 1931

France: 1944

Italy: 1946

India and Pakistan: 1947

Paraguay: 1961

Kenya: 1963

Switzerland: 1971

United Arab Emirates: 2006

Saudi Arabia: 2015

17 MARCH
SAINT PATRICK'S DAY

Saint Patrick is the patron saint of Ireland. However, he wasn't Irish, but probably either English, Welsh or Scottish! He was captured and enslaved by an Irish chieftain, escaped and fled the country, but later returned to Ireland to become a priest there. Legend says that he drove the snakes out of Ireland.

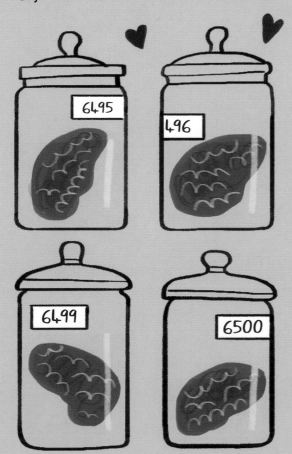

18 MARCH
ON THIS DATE

Alexiei Leonov became the first person to space walk on 18th March 1965. He was outside his spacecraft for more than 12 minutes, attached by a tether. He only just managed to get back inside the spacecraft because his spacesuit had inflated – he saved himself by opening a valve in his suit to deflate it enough to allow him to get back inside. His terrifying adventure didn't end there: the crew only just managed to stop the spacecraft from exploding, then the landing went wrong and they ended up 2,000 kilometres from where they were supposed to land, in the middle of a remote, freezing forest, surrounded by wolves and bears!

19 MARCH

The Duke of Burgundy was fond of extravagant banquets. In 1454, one of them lasted four days and included an enormous pie that was opened to reveal 28 musicians playing their instruments!

20 MARCH

Around the same time as the first hot-air balloons, parachutes were invented. In 1783 Jean Pierre Blanchard used a dog to test his own parachute design. Luckily, the dog was fine, and ten years later Blanchard used the parachute to successfully escape a balloon accident.

21 MARCH
WORLD POETRY DAY

The world's longest poem is the Mahabharata, sacred to the Hindu religion. It contains around 1.8 million words and tells the story of two sets of cousins at war with one another.

22 MARCH

The Barbie doll is the best-selling toy of all time. The doll was first revealed to the world in 1959 by her inventor and president of the Mattel toy company, Ruth Handler. The doll was named after Ruth Handler's daughter, Barbara.

23 MARCH

Saxons believed that to cure a wart you should rub the wart with a piece of meat, bury the meat, and as the meat rotted away, the wart would disappear. Wart-removing cream might be a better option!

24 MARCH

The Graff Pink is a rare pink diamond, and the most expensive jewel ever sold – it was bought for US $46 million.

25 MARCH

The ancient Minoan civilisation on the island of Crete practised bull-leaping – jumping over a bull by grabbing the animal's horns and somersaulting over its back – probably as part of a religious ritual. In Spain and southwest France, people still leap over bulls today.

26 MARCH

The biggest meteorite in the world was found in Namibia. It measures 2.73 x 2.3 metres – that's bigger than a cow – weighs more than 60 tonnes, and is made of iron and nickel.

27 MARCH

As far back as the Stone Age, people all over the world practised drilling holes in the skull, known as trepanning. No one knows why, but it must have given people a headache. The earliest head-drilling operation we know about dates back 7,000 years! Amazingly, they were on to something – some modern medical procedures involve a similar method.

28 MARCH

The peregrine falcon is the world's fastest animal. It can reach speeds of up to 320 kilometres per hour as it zooms towards the earth in a death-defying hunting dive called a stoop. The falcon crashes into its prey at such speed that the prey is stunned or even killed. The bird then swipes it out of the air and flies off to eat it.

29 MARCH

In Alaska in 1958, an earthquake toppled tonnes of rock into a narrow inlet, creating a giant wave 520 metres high – that's taller than the Empire State Building. It was the tallest wave ever recorded.

30 MARCH

Do you know someone who snores? A medical study suggests that playing the didgeridoo regularly helps reduce snoring, because of the special breathing techniques needed to play it.

31 MARCH

A snake's forked tongue picks up tiny particles in the air and transfers them to the roof of its mouth, where it can taste and smell them. The tongue has evolved into a fork because it's the perfect shape to pick up the most information possible, allowing the snake to track down its prey as quickly as possible.

1 APRIL
APRIL FOOL'S DAY

One of the best April Fool's jokes was played by British astronomer Patrick Moore in 1974. On BBC Radio 2, Moore announced that at 9.47am Pluto would pass behind Jupiter, and this would lessen the Earth's gravity. He said that if people jumped in the air at the right moment, they'd experience floating. Hundreds of listeners phoned in to say they'd felt the effect, and one woman said that she and her friends had floated up off their chairs and drifted around the room.

2 APRIL

Diamonds are worth more money than any other precious stone. The ancient Chinese didn't think much of them, though. They used them to cut jade, but not as jewellery or decoration!

3 APRIL

DNA, or deoxyribonucleic acid, found inside cells, is the instruction manual for every cell in your body. Almost all of your DNA is the same as everyone else's, less than one per cent is different, but that's what makes you unique.

4 APRIL

John Logie Baird is famous for inventing the television (although later electronic TVs weren't based on his invention, which was mechanical). He also invented pneumatic shoes, which burst, and a rustless razor.

5 APRIL

Scientists estimate that there are 10^{31} bacteria alive on Earth – that's a ten with thirty-one zeroes after it! The number is 100 million times the number of stars in the Universe that can be observed from Earth.

6 APRIL

The ancient Maya people, who lived in Mexico and Central America, had some unusual beauty tips. They liked crossed eyes, so they tried to train babies' eyes to turn inwards, they filed teeth into points, zigzags and other shapes and had semi-precious stones set into them, and they liked long, sloping foreheads, so they sometimes strapped pieces of wood to babies' heads to flatten them.

7 APRIL

There are daytime fireworks as well as the better-known night-time ones. Rather than bursting into colourful explosions, daytime fireworks put more emphasis on noise (they are deafening) and smoke. They're popular in Spain, especially in the city of Valencia.

9 APRIL

The languages spoken in the most countries:

- ✖ English: 57 countries
- ✖ French: 33 countries
- ✖ Arabic: 23 countries
- ✖ Spanish: 21 countries
- ✖ Portuguese: 7 countries

8 APRIL

Orangutans eat mostly fruit, but they've been spotted catching and eating cute little monkey-like creatures called slow lorises.

10 APRIL

The languages spoken by the most people:

✗ Spanish: around 332 million speakers

✗ Mandarin Chinese: around 885 million speakers

✗ English: around 322 million speakers

✗ Arabic: around 246 million speakers

✗ Hindustani: around 182 million speakers

11 APRIL

The first ever penalty kick in World Cup history was taken in 1930 by Carlos Vidal of Chile. Alex Thépot of France saved it, and became the first World Cup goalkeeper to save a penalty.

12 APRIL

Microwave ovens were invented during the Second World War, after a scientist working on radar noticed that his microwave-producing radar set had melted his chocolate bar!

13 APRIL

Hippopotamuses are the third largest land animals (after elephants and rhinos). Despite their cuddly appearance, they're very dangerous creatures and have killed people. They have huge, tusk-like teeth up to 60 centimetres long. You should never get between a hippo and its baby, or block its path to water – in fact it's a good idea to steer clear of them altogether!

14 APRIL

If you'd had whooping cough in the 1800s, you might have tried swallowing a buttered spider to cure it. Yum!

15 APRIL

Istanbul, in Turkey, is one of very few cities in the world to span two continents: it's partly in Europe and partly in Asia.

16 APRIL

Hatshepsut was the first ancient Egyptian female pharaoh. She dressed as a man and wore a false beard to carry out her ceremonial duties!

17 APRIL

Cows have four parts to their stomachs. The largest part, called the rumen, can hold 50 litres of partially digested food. Food from the rumen is regurgitated and rechewed before being swallowed again. A cow can spend eight hours a day chewing regurgitated food!

18 APRIL

Born in Liverpool in 1882, Anna Pepper was given 26 first names, one for every letter of the alphabet. Her full name was Anna Bertha Cecelia Diana Emily Fanny Gertrude Hypatia Inez Jane Kate Louisa Maud Nora Ophelia Prudence Quince Rebecca Starkey Teresa Ulysis Venus Winifred Xenophon Yetty Zeus Pepper. What a mouthful!

19 APRIL

The Vikings believed in lots of different gods. The chief god, Odin, was the god of magic, poetry and war. The goddess of love was Freyja, who wept golden tears when she was sad. Thor was the god of the sky, thunder and lightning, who wore iron gloves and a magic belt, and protected the home of the gods with a hammer that could smash mountains.

20 APRIL

After his death, Albert Einstein's brain was studied by Dr William Harvey, to see if there was anything unusual about it that could explain the great scientist's genius. Harvey kept the preserved brain in two jars for 40 years, every so often cutting off slices to send to brain specialists around the world. Harvey found the brain to be pretty normal, but other studies have found that there are unusual grooves in part of the brain. Whether Einstein was born like that, or whether his brain developed differently through his life, nobody knows.

21 APRIL

Japanese spider crabs are enormous – their long, spindly legs can span 3.8 metres – the size of a small car.

22 APRIL

The Mongolian leader Genghis Khan conquered more land than Alexander the Great and Napoleon put together. His Mongol Empire continued to grow after he died, and became the second biggest in the world ever.

23 APRIL

In the 1600s, Archbishop Ussher spent ages working out that God created the first living things – Adam and Eve – at 9.00 am on Sunday 23rd October 4004 BC. Unfortunately, he didn't know that the first cities had existed long before that!

24 APRIL

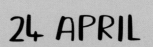

Ladybirds have a surprising weapon: they have poisonous knees! They release a toxic fluid when they're threatened to deter predators.

25 APRIL

Mount Everest, at 8,848 metres high, is the world's highest mountain. It was first climbed in 1953 by Edmund Hilary and Tenzing Norgay, and since then more than 4,000 people have made it to the top. The youngest person to have climbed Everest is Jordan Romero, aged 13, in 2010, and the oldest is Yuichiro Miura, who was a sprightly 80 years old when he reached the highest peak in the world, in 2013.

26 APRIL

Scientists have discovered that herring communicate by farting. The underwater bubbles send a message to other herrings that help the fish group together in shoals at night.

27 APRIL
ON THIS DATE

On 27 April 1791, Samuel Morse, inventor of Morse Code, was born. His invention used a series of dots and dashes to represent letters of the alphabet. A skilled listener or observer can understand Morse Code, without using special equipment. It looks complicated and time-consuming, but Morse code experts can receive and transmit messages at least as fast as texting.

28 APRIL

All the world's rivers and lakes put together only account for 25% of the fresh water in the world. The rest is frozen in glaciers. If they melted, the sea level would rise by about 70 metres, and some countries, including parts of the UK, would be underwater.

29 APRIL

Vladimir Lenin, one of the leaders of the Russian Revolution, died in the early days of communist Russia, in 1924. His body was embalmed and placed in a glass coffin, and you can still see it on display in Moscow today.

30 APRIL

Wombats produce cube-shaped poo. The wombat has a long digestive process, which dries out the poo, and ridges in the animal's intestine make it into cubes. The shape is an advantage because it stops the poo from rolling off logs and rocks, where wombats often deposit it to show other wombats that they live nearby.

1 MAY

Bio-buses run on biomethane, generated by sewage and food waste. The first one in the UK travelled between Bath and Bristol Airport in 2014. You can ride on a bio-bus knowing you've done your bit to fuel it!

2 MAY

Five unusual royal nicknames:

- Boleslaw the Curly was a Polish king
- Sancho the Fat ruled Leon in Spain
- Ordono the Wicked ruled Leon after Sancho
- Joanna the Mad was a Spanish queen, who was married to...
- Philip the Handsome

3 MAY

The Great Pyramid at Giza in Egypt was finished around 2560 BC. It remained the tallest building in the world until Lincoln Cathedral was built in 1300, around 3,860 years later.

4 MAY

Our galaxy, the Milky Way, is spinning as it travels through the universe. It makes a complete rotation once every 200 million years.

5 MAY

The sperm whale has the largest brain (and the largest head to fit it in) of any animal that's ever lived. It can hold its breath for 90 minutes and dive down nearly two kilometres. Sperm whales prey on animals including giant squid.

6 MAY

In the very early days of cars, Britain's Red Flag Act required all cars to have two people on board, keep to a speed limit of 6.5 kilometres per hour, and have someone walking in front of the car waving a red flag as a warning. It would almost have been quicker to walk! The act was withdrawn in 1896, when the speed limit was increased to 22 kilometres per hour.

7 MAY
ON THIS DATE

On 7 May 2005, a Time Traveller Convention was held at the Massachusetts Institute of Technology in 2005. It hoped to attract visitors from the future, but didn't succeed, although 300 people did attend. The event continues to be advertised so that future time travellers might go!

8 MAY

The closest star to Earth (apart from the Sun) is Proxima Centauri, and it's a very long way away: 4.22 light years. A light year is the distance light travels in one year, so 4.22 light years is the same as 39,953,525,879,212 kilometres.

9 MAY

Exploding Head Syndrome isn't quite as bad as it sounds. Usually during sleep, sufferers hear a very loud noise, like a gunshot. It's very alarming, but not dangerous.

10 MAY

A tarsier is a small, nocturnal primate. It has huge eyes for seeing in the dark, and each one is bigger than its brain!

11 MAY

The VW Beetle holds the world record for the best-selling single model of any car. It kept the same basic design from 1938 until 2003, and more than 21.5 million of them were sold.

12 MAY

The world's six tallest man-made structures:

13 MAY

In the early 1900s, wealthy Londoners sometimes had their homes cleaned with the newly invented horse-drawn, petrol-driven vacuum cleaner. Ladies even threw vacuum cleaner parties to impress their friends!

The Burj Khalifa in Dubai, United Arab Emirates: 830 metres

Tokyo Skytree, Tokyo, Japan: 634 metres

Abraj Al Bait Towers, Mecca, Saudi Arabia: 601 metress

14 MAY

There are 88 official constellations. Most of them were named thousands of years ago after characters and animals from mythology, for example, Orion the Hunter, the beautiful queen Cassiopeia, and Leo the lion. Some were named in the eighteenth century and have duller names: the Drafting Compass and the Air Pump are two of them.

INS Kattabomman, Tirunelveli, India: 471 metres

Lualualei VLF Transmitter, Lualualei, Hawaii: 458 metres

Petronas Towers, Kuala Lumpur, Malaysia: 452 metres

15 MAY

Three unusual laws:

• In France, it's against the law to call a pig Napoleon.

• In the United Kingdom, Members of Parliament are forbidden from wearing a suit of armour in the House of Commons.

• In Indonesia, owners of pet monkeys have to have photo ID for the monkey.

16 MAY

A giraffe's neck can measure up to 2.5 metres long, and the animal itself can stand six metres tall. Giraffes also have very long tongues, up to half a metre long, which are blue!

17 MAY

Maximilien Robespierre became one of the leaders of the French Revolution in 1791. His time in power is known as the Reign of Terror because he sent approximately 30,000 people to be executed by guillotine.

18 MAY

Some of the world's oldest art is found on cave walls in El Castillo Cave in northern Spain – it's been dated to 40,000 years ago. However, the oldest engravings are even older than that: 540,000 years ago human-like creatures (possibly our early ancestors), carved triangular lines on to a shell using a shark's tooth!

19 MAY

The Pan-American Highway is the longest drivable road in the world. The road runs all the way from North America to South America, apart from a gap of 100 kilometres to make way for the rainforest. It spans 18 countries and is 48,000 kilometres long.

20 MAY

In the nineteenth century people in Europe were fascinated by Egyptian mummies, but they didn't always treat them with respect. Bits of mummy were mixed with dye to make an artist's paint called 'Mummy Brown', and they were also used to make medicines. In 'unrollings', mummies were unwrapped and taken apart while an audience watched.

21 MAY

Samurai warriors had some unusual weapons, including the tessen, a fan made out of iron so that it was nice and heavy for bashing people over the head. (This is not a good idea!)

22 MAY
ON THIS DATE

The strongest earthquake ever recorded happened in Valdivia, Chile, on 22 May 1960. It scored 9.5 on the Richter scale. The earthquake caused tsunamis that rushed to land in faraway Hawaii and Japan, causing massive destruction there too.

23 MAY

The explorer Captain James Cook sailed all over the world and mapped New Zealand, Australia and Hawaii. He outstayed his welcome in Hawaii and was attacked and killed. When his crew asked for his body to be returned, they found that it had been cut into pieces. Cook's remains were buried at sea.

24 MAY

In many parts of the world you can buy insect snacks including grasshoppers, locusts, crickets and beetles. In parts of Africa, termites are roasted and eaten by the handful. They're much more nutritious than a bag of crisps!

25 MAY

The cheetah is the fastest animal on land. It speeds along at up to 114 kilometres per hour as it sprints after its prey. The cheetah can cover seven metres in a single bound!

26 MAY

There are around 100 billion nerve cells (neurons) in your brain, all linked together and carrying electrical signals to pass on information throughout your body. They do this every minute of the day, even while you're asleep!

27 MAY

The very first cars used tillers, like the ones used to steer boats. The first record of a steering wheel was in a Paris to Rouen race in 1894. Alfred Vacheron used a wheel to turn his car, and his idea caught on.

28 MAY

Watch out for Lonomia obliqua, a big hairy moth caterpillar that lives in South America. It has been known to kill people who touch it – its hairs inject poison!

29 MAY

The heaviest hailstones ever recorded pelted down on Bangladesh in 1986, each weighing one kilogram. The largest hailstone ever measured was 17.8 centimetres in diameter, and fell on Nebraska, USA.

30 MAY

A mangrove monkey's huge stomach weighs as much as the rest of its body put together!

31 MAY

These gases are commonly found in farts, although every fart is slightly different! Only about one per cent of a fart is responsible for the whiffy smell.

✖ METHANE
Not all farts contain methane, which is another flammable gas.

✖ NITROGEN
This is the gas that makes up most of the air we breathe, and it doesn't smell.

✖ HYDROGEN
Hydrogen is flammable, and combines with sulphides to make rotten-egg-smelling hydrogen sulphide.

✖ CARBON DIOXIDE
This is the same gas we breathe out.

✖ OXYGEN
There is very little oxygen in farts, which is also found in the air we breathe.

1 JUNE

Locusta was a famous female poisoner in ancient Rome. She was responsible for the poisoned mushrooms that killed Emperor Claudius in AD 54 (on the orders of Claudius's wife), and she also supplied the poison that killed Emperor Nero's stepbrother Britannicus (on the orders of Nero). Eventually, Locusta was executed after Nero's death.

2 JUNE

In 1782 a woman started laughing at a performance of The Beggar's Opera, a comedy musical, and didn't stop laughing until she died the following morning. There have been other recorded cases of people dying from laughing: one of them at a television comedy programme called The Goodies in 1975. The cause of the laughter was a man dressed in a kilt using a set of bagpipes to fend off an attacking black pudding. Afterwards, the man's wife wrote to the TV company thanking them for making her husband's last moments so hilarious.

3 JUNE

In Sardinia, some people eat the delicacy casu marzu, or 'maggot cheese'. It's made by leaving sheep's cheese out for flies to land on and lay their eggs, and then waiting for the maggots to hatch. Some people prefer to remove the eight-millimetre-long maggots before eating the cheese, while others like to leave them in!

4 JUNE

Prince Arthur, Queen Victoria's son, accidentally shot his brother-in-law, Prince Christian, in the eye while they were hunting. Prince Christian used a glass eye after that, and would often show people his glass eye collection – his favourite was a bloodshot one.

5 JUNE

In 1859, Jean Francois Gravelet crossed the Niagara Gorge, 1.5 kilometres downstream of the Niagara Falls, on a tightrope suspended 50 metres above the surface of the water. The crossing was a distance of 335 metres, and he made eight crossings altogether: including one on stilts, one pushing a wheelbarrow, and another carrying his manager on his back!

6 JUNE

Box jellyfish are some of the world's most venomous creatures, and kill people swimming in the sea every year. Their long, trailing tentacles (up to three metres of them) inject a powerful venom that's so painful it can stop a person's heart.

7 JUNE

Many of the world's most revolutionary inventions have come from China. The Chinese invented paper (and paper money), gunpowder (and fireworks), printing, silk, and the compass.

8 JUNE

The world's first automobile didn't run on petrol but steam. The *Fardier á vapeur* (steam cart) was built by Nicolas-Joseph Cugnot in 1769. It was big and bulky, and very slow.

9 JUNE

Tinned food was invented in 1810, 45 years before tin openers! Before that, people struggled with hammers, chisels, bayonets, and all sorts of dangerous tools. The first tin openers weren't much better, and it was over a hundred years before tinned food could be opened without going to a huge amount of bother.

10 JUNE

The original London Bridge was completed in 1831, but needed to be replaced in the twentieth century to support modern traffic. A wealthy American, Robert P McCulloch, bought it for £1,000,000, and had it transported to Lake Havasu City in Arizona, where it was reconstructed stone by stone. It was finished in 1971, and is still the biggest structure ever moved and the biggest antique ever sold.

11 JUNE

The world's smallest insect is the fairy wasp. An adult is just 0.44 millimetres long.

12 JUNE

The world's smallest frog (and the world's smallest backboned animal) is the Amau frog, which is just 8 millimetres long when it's fully grown.

13 JUNE

The world's smallest bird is the bee hummingbird, at just 5 centimetres long (it's a centimetre longer than the world's biggest bee). It's only half the size of the world's biggest insect.

14 JUNE

The Nazca Lines in Peru are huge drawings scratched into the ground showing geometric patterns, spirals and animals. They were made by the Nazca people, who lived there between 300 BC and AD 800. It's a mystery why the drawings are so big when the Nazca couldn't see them from high up – the whole drawings can only be seen fully from a height of 300 metres.

15 JUNE

The first toilets that flushed were built more than 4,000 years ago, in the Indus Valley and Minoan civilisations.

16 JUNE
ON THIS DATE

Valentina Tereshkova became the first woman in space on 16th June 1963. Her husband was also a cosmonaut, and their baby was the first person to be born whose parents had both travelled into space.

17 JUNE

Purple foxglove leaves contain a powerful poison called digitalis. Eating just a handful of the leaves can be fatal.

18 JUNE

The 240-page-long Voynich Manuscript is a complete mystery. It dates back from the 1400s and is written in an unknown language and alphabet that no one has been able to decipher. It includes pictures of plants that no one can identify, and mysterious circular drawings, among other things. Although many have tried, no one has been able to work out what any of it means, and it continues to baffle experts and code-breakers around the world!

19 JUNE

Viking Lief Ericsson was probably the first European to sail across the Atlantic to North America, almost 500 years before Christopher Columbus. Around AD 1000, Ericsson landed in Newfoundland, off the coast of Canada, and began a settlement there.

20 JUNE

Mammoth Cave in Kentucky is the longest cave system in the world to be discovered so far – it's 580 kilometres long, but probably much more of it is still undiscovered. Human remains dating back thousands of years have been found in its dark chambers.

21 JUNE

Rampaging barbarian warrior Attila the Hun fought the Romans in the last days of the Roman Empire, but in 453 his rampaging days came to an end: he died on one of his wedding nights (he married lots of times), after having a nosebleed. That's the story, but he might have been murdered...

22 JUNE

The biggest rodents of all time (as far as we know) were giant pacaranas, from South America, which died out two million years ago. These cow-sized creatures could be three metres long and 1.5 metres at the shoulder, they had 30-centimetre-long teeth and weighed about a tonne.

23 JUNE

Birch polypore mushrooms are very useful. They're edible, are said to have medicinal uses, can be used to sharpen razors, and also make good hats – the fibre of the mushroom is a bit like felt. An all round multipurpose mushroom!

24 JUNE

Puerto Lopez de Micay in Colombia is the wettest place on Earth. On average, 12,890 millimetres of rain falls there every year. If you're planning a trip, pack your wellies!

25 JUNE

The most deadly disease event in history was an outbreak of flu. It started in 1918, at the end of the First World War, and spread all around the world, killing 40 million people – even more people than died in the war.

26 JUNE

In the past, sailors on long sea voyages often got the disease scurvy, which made their teeth drop out (among other horrible symptoms) and could be fatal. Eating fresh fruit and vegetables containing vitamin C prevents you from catching the disease and from the 1740s sailors took lemons, limes and pickled vegetables on their sea voyages.

27 JUNE

The fastest-swimming fish is the sailfish, which speeds through the sea at 110 kilometres per hour – almost as fast as a speed boat!

28 JUNE

In peat bogs, chemicals and a lack of oxygen preserves organic material, and ancient dead bodies are sometimes found in them. The oldest one ever found is known as Koelbjerg Woman, found in a bog in Denmark – it's about 10,000 years old!

29 JUNE

During an average lifetime, your heart will beat about 2.21 billion times, and you'll take around 672 million breaths.

30 JUNE

Ancient Egyptian mummy makers took great care with the preparation of dead bodies in order to mummify them, and kept the internal organs in special jars. However, they didn't think the brain was important for the afterlife, and threw it away!

1 JULY

Susanna Montgomery, Countess of Eglintoune, was an eccentric Scottish aristocrat in the 1700s. She kept hundreds of pet rats, which roamed freely around her house. She used to summon them to the dinner table by tapping on a panel in her dining room!

2 JULY

In the Middle Ages, pigs and other animals were sometimes put on trial and executed, usually for injuring or killing someone.

58075611
OINK

3 JULY

The Golden Buddha in Bankok, Thailand, is the biggest golden statue in the world, at three metres tall and 5.5 tonnes in weight. It was made in the 1200s or 1300s, but it was plastered over in the 1700s to protect it from looters. It lay forgotten for 200 years until, in the 1950s, a chunk of plaster chipped off as the statue was being moved, revealing the gold underneath!

4 JULY
INDEPENDENCE DAY

The United States celebrates its birthday today, after it became independent from Britain. The final wording of the Declaration of Independence was agreed on 4 July 1776.

5 JULY

These four snakes are probably the most deadly in the world. Even though there are snakes with more powerful venom, these snakes are aggressive and make their homes near people. Between them they kill tens of thousands of people every year, mostly throughout South Asia.

- ✖ Indian cobra
- ✖ Common krait
- ✖ Russell's viper
- ✖ Saw-scaled viper

6 JULY

Women weren't allowed to join the navy in the eighteenth and nineteenth centuries, but Mary Ann Riley and Ann Hopping fought with Nelson at the Battle of the Nile in 1798, and Jane Townshend fought at the Battle of Trafalgar in 1805, all of them disguised as men. Years later they asked Queen Victoria for medals, like the ones the male sailors had been given, but the queen refused.

7 JULY

The biggest reptile in the world is the saltwater crocodile. It can reach up to seven metres long and is extremely fierce. Around 60 people are eaten by saltwater crocodiles every year, usually while fishing in creeks. The crocodiles don't go looking for people to eat, but will happily munch on any animal they happen to find, and can catch.

8 JULY

On average, the sea is about four kilometres deep, but the deepest part of the ocean, the Mariana Trench, is almost 11 kilometres deep. If you dropped Mount Everest into it, there would still be 1.6 kilometres of water above its peak! The deepest part of the Mariana Trench is called Challenger Deep. Only three people have ever explored it – Jacques Piccard and Don Walsh in 1960, and James Cameron in 2012. They used highly specialised submarines, because the pressure at that depth is so great.

9 JULY

An octopus has three hearts, nine brains, and blue blood.

10 JULY

Painter, inventor and all-round genius Leonardo da Vinci invented 'flotation shoes' in the 1500s. The shoes were meant to walk on water, and were tried out successfully in the 1800s!

11 JULY

The Dead Sea is one of the world's deepest lakes. It's nearly ten times as salty as the sea, which allows you to easily float on top of the water!

12 JULY

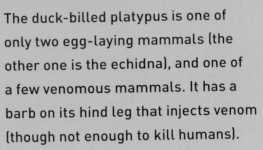

The duck-billed platypus is one of only two egg-laying mammals (the other one is the echidna), and one of a few venomous mammals. It has a barb on its hind leg that injects venom (though not enough to kill humans).

13 JULY

The word atom comes from an ancient Greek word meaning 'uncuttable'. Democritus, an ancient Greek philosopher, came up with the word to describe the smallest particles of which everything else is made. But now we know that there are smaller things than atoms after all...

14 JULY

There's enough iron in an average human body to make a 7.5 centimetre nail, and enough phosphorus to make 220 match heads.

16 JULY

Roman Emperor Caligula had a favourite horse called Incitatus. According to the Roman historian Suetonius, he gave it a marble stable with an ivory manger and had gold leaf mixed into its oats. Caligula had even planned to make it a politician!

15 JULY

Lamprechtsofen Cave in Austria is 1,632 metres deep, one of the deepest caves in the world. It was walled up in 1701 to stop people searching for legendary treasure. When it was reopened in the twentieth century, the bones of dead treasure hunters were found.

17 JULY

Alex, an African Grey parrot at the University of Arizona, could speak, count up to six, tell what things were made of by testing them with his beak, ask his trainer for food and water, and say what shape and colour different objects were.

18 JULY

The world's most dangerous spider is the Brazilian wandering spider. It's aggressive, can jump, and its venomous bite can kill an adult unless it's treated quickly. The spiders live in South America but have been known to travel the world in bunches of bananas.

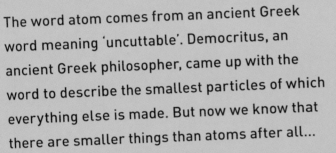

19 JULY

Roman Emperor Claudius made a law allowing people to fart at banquets, because he was concerned that holding them in damaged people's health!

N. ARMSTRONG

20 JULY
ON THIS DATE

On 20 July 1969, Neil Armstrong and Buzz Aldrin became the first human beings to walk on the surface of the Moon. Only 12 people have ever set foot on the Moon, two in each of six Moon missions. One of them, Alan Shepard, took the opportunity to hit a golf ball on the Moon's surface – it travelled for more than two kilometres and took over a minute to land, because of the Moon's low gravity.

B. ALDRIN

21 JULY

Hippos have the horrible habit of twirling their tails as they poo, creating a foul-smelling shower to mark their territory.

22 JULY

The smallest production car ever made is the Peel P50, which is still being produced today. It can only carry one person, and has one door and one headlight. It's around 140 centimetres long, 100 centimetres wide and 120 centimetres in height.

23 JULY

The flower of the rafflesia measures almost a metre across and smells terrible. It's also known as the stinking corpse lily, which gives you an idea of its horrible whiff. The smell attracts flies, which pollinate the plant.

24 JULY

The longest mountain range on Earth lies mostly under the sea: the Mid-Atlantic Ridge runs down the middle of the Atlantic Ocean, from north to south, and is more than 60,000 kilometres long. Two of the Earth's tectonic plates – giant chunks of the Earth's crust – meet there, and are moving apart at roughly the rate your fingernails grow.

25 JULY

A starfish can grow an entire new body from just one of its arms (known as 'rays') and a small piece of the centre of its body.

26 JULY

Male humpback whales sing long and complicated songs to one another. Songs are often repeated over and over again, and sometimes several whales sing the same song. Over time, the songs change, with new bits added to them. The sounds can travel for thousands of kilometres through the ocean! No one is quite sure why the whales sing, but it might be to do with attracting a female humpback.

27 JULY

In 2010 there was an enormous traffic jam on China National Highway 110. It was 100 kilometres long and lasted ten days, with cars moving about one kilometre per day.

28 JULY

Austrailian Aborigines didn't use maps. Instead they sang songs about local landmarks to find their way around.

29 JULY

Horned lizards can spurt blood from their eyeballs to scare off predators.

30 JULY

If you want to compliment someone's cooking in Portugal, kiss your index finger then squeeze your ear – apparently, this means the food you've just eaten is very tasty!

31 JULY

The longest ship ever built was the Seawise Giant (the ship had several different names in its lifetime, including the Happy Giant). Stood on its end, it would have been one and a half times the height of London's tallest building, the Shard! It was so enormous that there were lots of ports it couldn't get to, and it couldn't navigate the English Channel, the Suez Canal or the Panama Canal. It was finally dismantled in India in 2010.

1 AUGUST

The smallest horse in the world is smaller than a Labrador dog: Thumbelina is a miniature horse affected by dwarfism, and she is just 43 centimetres tall!

2 AUGUST

The Tower of London has a long history and lots of superstitions. One of them is that if the ravens that are kept there leave the Tower, the kingdom will fall. To guard against such a disaster, at least six ravens are kept at the Tower of London, looked after by the Ravenmaster.

3 AUGUST

The resurrection plant can survive for years without any water at all. In times of drought it dries up and goes into a sort of hibernation. When it's watered again – even if it's not for fifty years – it comes back to life.

4 AUGUST

The national sport in Bangladesh is called kabaddi. Two teams compete by sending one player at a time into the opposing team's territory, where they tag as many players as they can – but they have to do it while holding their breath, muttering 'kabaddi, kabaddi, kabaddi' at all times to prove they're not cheating.

5 AUGUST

Greenland sharks live in cold Arctic waters and swim very slowly. Apparently they age very slowly too – they're the oldest animals with a backbone, and can live up to about 400 years!

6 AUGUST
ON THIS DATE

Alexander Fleming was born on 6th August 1881. He discovered penicillin, and paved the way for modern antibiotics, which have saved millions of lives. His study of bacteria led to an unusual hobby: growing different coloured bacteria in Petri dishes to make pictures, including boxers, ballerinas and soldiers. He made a Union Jack bacteria picture for a visit from Queen Mary, but she wasn't interested in seeing it!

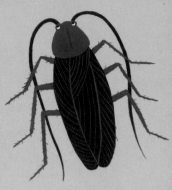

7 AUGUST

Venus Cloacina was the Roman goddess of sewers. In ancient Rome the main sewer had a very elaborate entrance, which was also Venus Cloacina's shrine.

8 AUGUST

Louis Braille was blinded in an accident when he was three years old. He later invented a system of reading by touch, instead of sight, using a system of raised dots on the page. After his death in 1854, his system, known as Braille, began to be used in France, where Braille had lived. Now it's used all over the world.

The Braille Alphabet

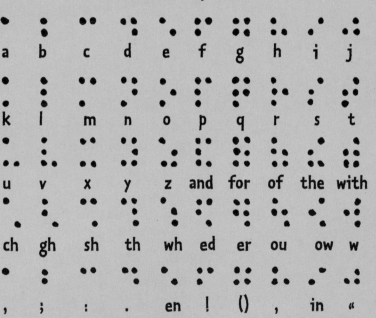

a b c d e f g h i j

k l m n o p q r s t

u v x y z and for of the with

ch gh sh th wh ed er ou ow w

, ; : . en ! () , in "

9 AUGUST

The bite of the blue-ringed octopus is deadly. When the animal's blue rings begin to glow it means it's getting ready to bite. The bite injects venom that can kill an adult human in minutes, though the creatures are only the size of a tennis ball. However, they're shy animals and very few human deaths have ever been recorded.

10 AUGUST

Six facts about cockroaches:

- There are more than 5,000 species of cockroach.
- The world's biggest cockroach is 15 centimetres long and has a wingspan of 30 centimetres.
- Cockroaches can hold their breath for 40 minutes.
- They can run at about 5.5 kilometres per hour – that's about as fast as you walk.
- They eat almost anything – glue, paper, their own cast-off skins, and sometimes each other!
- They're found everywhere in the world except at the North and South Poles.

11 AUGUST

Ten to fifteen thousand new icebergs form every year, as they break away from glaciers, mostly from Greenland in the Arctic, or Antarctica, in a process called 'calving'.

12 AUGUST

Chickens can survive a few seconds or minutes after their heads have been chopped off, running around like... headless chickens! One chicken in Colorado, USA, survived for much longer: Miracle Mike the Headless Chicken survived for 18 months without his head! Enough of his brain stem had been left to let him function almost normally.

13 AUGUST

The land surface area on Earth is 149 million km^2, while the water surface area is 361 million km^2! Human beings have only explored about 5% of the undersea world.

14 AUGUST

The stonefish is the most venomous fish in the world. Its camouflage makes it look very much like a stone on the sea bed. It preys on small fish and shrimps, and raises spines on its back to defend itself, which inject powerful venom that can kill a human being.

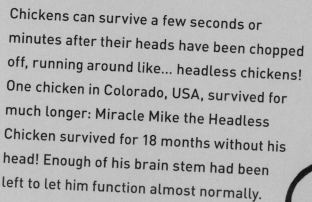

15 AUGUST
ON THIS DATE

Napoleon Bonaparte was born on 15th August 1769. As well as leading revolutionary France, Napoleon was also partly responsible for the invention of canned food: in 1795 he offered a reward to anyone who could come up with a way of preserving food, and 14 years later, Nicholas Appert demonstrated his sealed jars.

16 AUGUST

In 2005, someone paid £11,000 in an auction for one of Napoleon Bonaparte's teeth. If you're interested in the dental care of famous historical figures, Napoleon's toothbrush is on display at the Science Museum in London.

17 AUGUST

The brightest star in the sky (apart from our Sun) is Sirius, also known as the Dog Star. It's 24 times brighter than the Sun (but a lot further away, obviously!)

18 AUGUST

The howler monkey has the loudest call of all land animals – it can be heard for five kilometres. Under the sea, whales make even louder noises.

19 AUGUST

The Tomatina festival in Bunol, Spain, takes place in August. It involves a race to grab a ham from a greasy pole, then two hours of everyone throwing tomatoes at one another. At the end of it, the fire brigade hoses down the streets and everyone goes home for a bath.

20 AUGUST

Bacteria have been sent into space and survived the trip quite happily. Scientists are trying to discover whether they could survive on Mars. Some bacteria even live on electricity – unlike anything else on Earth!

21 AUGUST

The first ice lolly was made by accident in 1923 when lemonade salesman Frank Epperson left a glass of lemonade with a teaspoon in it on a windowsill on a freezing cold night. The next morning it had frozen solid. Removing the teaspoon, Epperson found he'd invented a tasty frozen treat!

22 AUGUST

Richard III was the last British king to be killed in battle. He died at the Battle of Bosworth on 22nd August 1485.

23 AUGUST

French musician Remy Bricka took nearly two months to walk 5,636 kilometres across the Atlantic in 1988 on 4.25-metre-long floating skis.

24 AUGUST

The colossal squid has never been seen alive, because it lives deep in the ocean. Occasionally, dead colossal squid wash up on the shore. The animal's eyes are the biggest in the world – each is the size of a football!

25 AUGUST

Christopher Columbus never set foot on the mainland of North America – he sailed to what are now known as the West Indies, so-called because Columbus thought the islands were off the coast of India. Columbus died thinking he'd sailed to Asia.

26 AUGUST

The Inca people of South America used gold and silver to make beautiful things but they didn't use it, or anything else, as money. They were one of the only civilizations that managed to do without money altogether.

27 AUGUST

Dreadnoughtus schrani is the biggest dinosaur, and the biggest land animal, that's been discovered so far. It was 24 metres long and weighed nearly 60 tonnes! But it's still nowhere near as big as the blue whale, which is the biggest animal that's ever lived and can weigh up to 180 tonnes – as much as 30 fully grown African elephants!

28 AUGUST

A medieval cure for a sore throat was to tie a string of worms around your neck. The theory was that as the worms died the sore throat would disappear. It didn't work, and hasn't caught on as a trend.

29 AUGUST

The world's most expensive, Kopi luwak, or civet coffee, is made from coffee beans that have been eaten by the weasel-like Asian palm civet and then retrieved from the animal's poo, partly digested.

30 AUGUST

When silk was first invented in China, the Chinese Emperor and his family were the only ones allowed to wear it. Silk was so valuable that for a while it was used as currency in China.

31 AUGUST

Insects called springtails live in the soil all over the world. There are more of them than of any other type of insect – thousands for every square metre of land. If you put them all together, they'd weigh more than all the humans on the planet!

1 SEPTEMBER

Madagascar is the fourth largest island in the world. It's home to 250,000 different animal species, 70% of which are found nowhere else on Earth. Ninety per cent of the island's 14,000 plant species are only found on Madagascar.

2 SEPTEMBER

The goliath bird-eating spider, from South America, is the biggest spider in the world. Its maximum leg span is 30 centimetres – the size of a dinner plate! It has 2.5-centimetre-long fangs, which can deliver a nasty bite, but thankfully don't inject enough venom to kill a person.

3 SEPTEMBER

The Voyager spacecraft, Voyager 1 and 2, set off on their journeys into space in 1977. Both spacecraft carried gold-plated copper discs containing information about life on Earth, including greetings in different languages, scenes of Earth, pictures, and music, which might one day tell other space travellers about our planet. Voyager 1 and 2 have travelled further than anything else from Earth, and are still sending back information.

4 SEPTEMBER

Ancient Greek thinkers Aristotle, Socrates, Plato and Pythagoras were all vegetarians and spoke out against cruelty to animals.

5 SEPTEMBER

Australia has the world's only herds of wild camels. They were imported to Australia from the Middle East in the 1800s.

6 SEPTEMBER

Roman Emperor Commodus sometimes fought in Rome's bloodthirsty games as a gladiator, to show how tough he was. However, he made sure his opponents' weapons were made of lead so that he always won. At one event, he cut an ostrich's head off and displayed it to the politicians who were watching as a warning of what he might easily do to them.

8 SEPTEMBER

Football in the Middle Ages was a dangerous sport: huge football games were played between entire villages, in which players tried to kick a blown-up pig's bladder into the other team's church. Edward II of England banned football in London in 1314 because he believed it caused a disturbance and 'many evils'.

9 SEPTEMBER

Mount Vesuvius in Italy is considered to be the world's most dangerous volcano because it's only nine kilometres from the city of Naples, which is home to three million people. It erupted in AD 79, covering the cities of Pompeii and Herculaneum in choking ash and killing thousands of people. Since then, it's erupted 30 times.

7 SEPTEMBER

The world's fastest roller coaster is called Formula Rossa. It accelerates to a stomach-lurching top speed of 239 kilometres per hour in just five seconds, using a hydraulic launch system, and lasts a thrilling one and a half minutes. If you're brave enough to try it, the roller coaster is at Ferrari World in Abu Dhabi, United Arab Emirates.

YE OLDE GOOOAL!!

10 SEPTEMBER

In the ocean depths, hydrothermal vents shoot hot chemicals from deep in the Earth into the sea. Pompeii worms live inside tubes burrowed into the vents, at temperatures of 80°C and under intense pressure.

11 SEPTEMBER

Hurricanes are storms in which the winds are faster than 118 kilometres per hour. They're caused when warm air rises quickly and is pushed aside as it cools, making it spin. Hurricanes, typhoons and cyclones all mean the same thing, but the names are used in different areas: in the Atlantic and northeast Pacific it's a hurricane; in the northwest Pacific it's a typhoon; and in the South Pacific and Indian Ocean it's a cyclone.

12 SEPTEMBER

When you're eight years old, your brain is already the same size as it's going to be when you're an adult!

13 SEPTEMBER

In 480 BC Persian emperor Xerxes was planning to invade Greece. He gathered an army and navy and made bridges out of boats across the Hellespont, the narrow stretch of sea that links the Mediterranean with the Sea of Marmaris. When a storm destroyed the bridges, Xerxes was so cross that he had the sea whipped with chains to teach it a lesson!

14 SEPTEMBER

Before modern dentistry, people had a lot more problems with their teeth. They treated them with grim-sounding cures including strapping a toad to your jaw, picking bones out of wolf poo and wearing them, and washing your teeth in tortoise's blood three times a year. Going to the dentist doesn't sound so bad now, does it?

15 SEPTEMBER

Scientists have created a drug that stops blood from clotting, using the saliva of vampire bats. It's called Draculin, after the vampire Count Dracula, from the novel by Bram Stoker.

16 SEPTEMBER

Albert Einstein is famous for his theory of relativity and showing that $E = mc^2$ (i.e. that there's an enormous amount of energy locked up inside atoms). But he's not so famous for inventing a fridge: Einstein and his former student, Leo Szilard, took out a patent on the fridge in 1930.

17 SEPTEMBER

If you've ever tried skimming stones, you'll be amazed to know that the world record is 88 skips – achieved by expert stone-skimmer Kurt Steiner in 2013.

18 SEPTEMBER

Our noses and ears are made of cartilage, which is softer than bone. It continues to grow throughout our lives – so the older you get, the bigger your nose and ears grow!

19 SEPTEMBER
ON THIS DATE

On 19 September 1782, brothers Josef and Etienne Montgolfier tested their new invention, the hot-air balloon. The passengers on the historic first flight were a sheep, a cockerel and a duck, who flew successfully for 33 metres in ten minutes. (The duck would have done better without the balloon!)

20 SEPTEMBER

William Shakespeare invented around 1,700 of the words we use in English today, including bloodsucking, fairyland, hot-blooded, moonbeam, schoolboy, watchdog and zany!

21 SEPTEMBER

Most penguins mate for life, and return to the exact same nesting site year after year.

22 SEPTEMBER

The ancient Romans used pigeon poo to bleach their hair. How stylish!

23 SEPTEMBER

The green anaconda is the biggest snake in the world – it can grow up to nine metres long and weighs 230 kilogrammes. The snakes live in the rainforests of South America. They hunt large animals but aren't venomous, instead they kill their prey by squeezing it to death.

24 SEPTEMBER

Yuri Gagarin became the first person in space in 1961. He orbited the Earth in his spacecraft in 89 minutes and 34 seconds.

25 SEPTEMBER

Seven unusual phobias:

- Trichopathophobia (fear of hair)
- Peladophobia (fear of bald people)
- Genuphobia (fear of knees)
- Amathophobia (fear of dust)
- Hippopotomonstrosesquippedaliophobia (fear of long words, ironically)
- Bromidrosiphobia (fear of body odour)
- Pogonophobia (fear of beards)

26 SEPTEMBER

The longest bone in the human body is the thigh bone, or femur. The shortest bone in the human body is the stirrup, or stapes, in the middle ear.

27 SEPTEMBER

All snowflakes are different, but all of them have six sides. They all end up a bit different from one another because each snowflake follows a slightly different path down to the ground.

28 SEPTEMBER

The world's tallest mountain isn't Mount Everest – it's Mauna Kea in Hawaii and it's 10,205 metres tall, but most of it (6,000 metres) is under the sea. So Mount Everest is the highest mountain above ground.

29 SEPTEMBER
ON THIS DATE

On 29 September 1728 Horatio Nelson was born. He grew up to become a British naval hero. His most famous victory was at the Battle of Trafalgar, where he died aboard his ship, *HMS Victory*. His body was stored in a barrel of brandy or rum to preserve it until the ship got back to Britain. The story goes that when Nelson's body was removed, all the alcohol was found to have vanished – the sailors had made a hole in the barrel and sucked it out with a straw!

30 SEPTEMBER

As a defence against predators, the striped polecat plays dead and oozes foul-smelling, toxic liquid from its mouth, nose and bottom. The liquid can temporarily blind an attacker!

RUM

1 OCTOBER

American Dream was the longest limousine ever made, designed and built by Jay Ohrberg. It was 30 metres long, with 26 wheels, had its own jacuzzi and even a helipad! It was so difficult to manoeuvre that eventually it was abandoned and left to rust.

2 OCTOBER

A housefly can smell a piece of meat up to seven kilometres away.

3 OCTOBER

The Great Wall of China stretches for 7,300 kilometres altogether. It was built during the Ming dynasty (1368-1644) to keep out invaders from the north.

4 OCTOBER

There was a fashion for tiny waists for women in the nineteenth century, and many women wore corsets to pull in their waists. One Parisian woman's corset was so tight that it crushed her to death in 1859, and the fashion led to several other deaths as well. Thankfully, it is no longer a fashion!

5 OCTOBER

Geysers are hot springs formed in rocks that shoot giant spumes of water into the air every so often. There are around a thousand geysers in the world, about half of them in Yellowstone National Park in the United States. The others are in New Zealand, Iceland, Russia and Chile.

6 OCTOBER

Steamboat Geyser, in Yellowstone National Park, is the tallest active geyser in the world, shooting water up to 90 metres high. Eruptions can last for 40 minutes, and afterwards the geyser puffs out giant jets of steam for up to two days. It doesn't erupt at regular intervals, and it might not erupt at all for years or even decades.

7 OCTOBER
ON THIS DATE

On 7 October 2000, extreme skier Davo Karnicar skied down Mount Everest. He enjoyed the experience so much that he then skied down the highest peak on each of the other continents, ending with Antarctica's Vinson Massif in 2006.

8 OCTOBER

At the original Olympic Games in ancient Greece, athletes competed stark naked, and no women were allowed – either to take part or to watch. The Greek writer Pausanias tells the story of a woman who disguised herself as a male trainer, and sneaked into the games because she wanted to cheer on her athlete son. She was discovered when some of her clothing slipped down. Luckily the judges let her off the punishment – death! After that, trainers had to go to the games naked as well as the athletes.

9 OCTOBER

The pygmy marmoset, found in the rainforests of Central and South America, is the smallest monkey in the world. Its body is only 15 centimetres long – smaller than a guinea pig! The marmoset makes up for its short body with its long tail, which is 20 centimetres long.

10 OCTOBER

The Sahara is the world's biggest hot desert, and spans 11 countries. The highest temperature ever recorded in the Sahara was 58°C! The temperature at night drops dramatically – often by 25°C or even more.

11 OCTOBER

The biggest land mammal today is the elephant (and it's the biggest land animal too), but the biggest land mammal ever is the paraceratherium, a relative of modern rhinos. It weighed 20 tonnes – that's heavier than six male hippopotamuses!

12 OCTOBER

The ancient Romans had gods and goddesses for lots of things. These are some of their more unusual goddesses.

- Cardea, goddess of door hinges
- Bubona, goddess of cattle
- Mellona, goddess of bees
- Devera, goddess of brooms used to purify temples

13 OCTOBER

There are about three million pain sensors on the human body, most of them on the skin. Your fingertips and forehead are especially sensitive to pain. There are different receptors on your skin for pain, touch and temperature.

14 OCTOBER
ON THIS DATE

On 14 October 1829, the steam engine Rocket, designed by George Stephenson, won a competition to find a steam engine that could carry goods and passengers.

15 OCTOBER

Coco Chanel changed the fashion industry with her new designs. Her small shop in Paris became one of the biggest and most famous fashion houses ever. She started fashions for bobbed haircuts, trousers for women, and suntans. As a child she spent six years in an orphanage, but when she was rich and famous she lived the high life in the Ritz Hotel, for more than 30 years!

17 OCTOBER

Alexander the Great became king of Macedonia in 336 BC when he was 20, and began conquering more and more land. Eventually he stopped and celebrated his massive empire that now stretched from the Mediterranean to the Himalayas. After an especially big celebration, Alexander died suddenly, aged just 32.

16 OCTOBER

A skunk can fire foul-smelling liquid from glands underneath its tail for a distance of three metres. The oily, horrible-smelling stuff is hard to wash off, and the smell can last for days. Because of this whiffy trick, predators tend to steer clear of skunks.

18 OCTOBER

Fingernails grow between three and four times faster than toenails. No one's quite sure why, but it probably has to do with blood supply and circulation, and the fact that we use our fingers more than our toes.

19 OCTOBER

The Jivaro people of the Amazon rainforest chopped off their enemies' heads and then shrunk the heads as trophies of war. The Jivaro believed that this would stop the spirit of the dead person from taking revenge.

21 OCTOBER

On 21st October 1833, Alfred Nobel was born, the inventor of dynamite. In 1888, a French newspaper mistakenly thought he had died, and published an article calling him 'the merchant of death', because his explosive invention killed people more efficiently than ever before. After reading the article, Nobel decided that wasn't how he wanted to be remembered, and used his fortune to set up the Nobel Prizes, which are still awarded every year for outstanding achievements in physics, chemistry, medicine, literature, and for work in peace.

20 OCTOBER

The biggest and most complete T-rex fossil in the world is nicknamed 'Sue'. When it was auctioned in 1997, it sold for US $8.36 million to the Field Museum of Natural History in Chicago, USA, making 'Sue' the world's most expensive fossil.

ALFRED NOBEL

22 OCTOBER

As well as mummifying people, the ancient Egyptians made animals into mummies. Sometimes the animal mummies were pets that a person wanted to take with them to the afterlife, sometimes they were food for a person's journey to the afterlife, and sometimes they were mummified because they represented different gods. Ancient Egyptian animal mummies include cats, ibises and other types of bird, baboons, crocodiles, bulls, fish, mongooses, dogs, jackals, snakes, lizards, eels and beetles.

24 OCTOBER

Tardigrades, also known as water bears, are tiny animals only about half a millimetre long that live in water. The hard nuts of the animal kingdom, they can survive extreme temperatures, extreme pressure, radiation, and even drought! When there's no water for them to live in, they dehydrate and can stay that way for years, then carry on as normal when water returns. Dehydrated tardigrades have even been sent into the vacuum of space. When they were placed in water back on Earth, they were absolutely fine!

23 OCTOBER

The novel *Robinson Crusoe* by Daniel Defoe is based on a real-life desert-islander called Alexander Selkirk. He decided that the ship he was sailing in was too leaky to be safe, and said he'd rather stay on the island than continue in the ship without repairs. So he found himself marooned alone on a remote island 650 kilometres off the coast of Chile. He soon regretted his words – he was alone on the island for more than four years, surviving in a hut he made himself and on a diet of lobsters, wild goats and edible plants, until he was finally rescued.

25 OCTOBER

The world's most expensive chocolate is made in Connecticut, USA. It's called the Madeline au Truffe, made with a real truffle (a type of mushroom) and comes in a presentation box on a bed of sugar pearls. It costs US $250 – and that's just for one chocolate!

26 OCTOBER

Cassowaries are large, flightless birds found in Australia and New Guinea. They can be very territorial and sometimes attack people with their long, dagger-like claws.

27 OCTOBER

There were seven attempts to assassinate Queen Victoria, who ruled Britain from 1837-1901, but she wasn't harmed in any of them. Most involved pistols, but one man used a small stick to try to bash the queen on the head.

28 OCTOBER

Sir Richard Arkwright was a wigmaker who took up inventing when wigs went out of fashion. He invented spinning machines that completely changed the way textiles were made, and began the Industrial Revolution.

29 OCTOBER

Black mambas are some of the most feared snakes in Africa because they're deadly and fast-moving. They're usually light brown or grey in colour – they're called black mambas because the inside of their mouths is black.

30 OCTOBER
ON THIS DATE

On 30 October 1939, a radio music concert was interrupted by a 'news story' that said aliens from Mars had invaded New Jersey, USA, and were busy killing people with death rays from huge three-legged machines. The next morning, it was revealed that the 'news' was actually a play based on H. G. Wells's novel, *The War of the Worlds*. By that time, hundreds of people had fled their homes in a bid to escape the Martians.

31 OCTOBER
ALL HALLOW'S EVE (HALLOWE'EN)

Route 40 in western Maryland, USA, is supposed to be haunted by a black dog known as the Snarly Yow. Several drivers have spotted it in the middle of the road and thought they'd run it over. But when they stopped to investigate, there was nothing there . . .

1 NOVEMBER
THE DAY OF THE DEAD

The Day of the Dead is celebrated in Mexico. Families decorate the graves of their relatives with brightly coloured flowers. They make offerings of food and drink, to their deceased relatives, then families gather by the graveside for a picnic, remembering the dead and telling stories about them. The festival lasts for two or three days, and is a very happy occasion.

2 NOVEMBER

Shihuangdi, the first emperor of China, searched for an elixir of eternal life. He didn't find it, and in 210 BC he was buried in an enormous underground tomb along with thousands of almost life-sized terracotta models of warriors and horses to help him rule his empire after death. The terracotta army has survived more than 2,000 years.

3 NOVEMBER

Electric rays, or torpedo fish, were used by the ancient Greeks as a kind of anaesthetic. Doctors gave patients a shock from the animals to numb pain during childbirth or operations.

4 NOVEMBER

Some Vikings had interesting nicknames – we can only guess how they got them! They include Ragnar Hairy Breeches, Ulf the Unwashed, Keith Flatnose, and Einer Bellyshaker.

5 NOVEMBER
ON THIS DATE

In Britain, people still celebrate Guy Fawkes Night on 5 November with fireworks and bonfires. Guy Fawkes and his co-conspirators planned to blow up the Houses of Parliament in London in what became known as the Gunpowder Plot. It used to be a criminal offence in England not to celebrate the capture of Guy Fawkes!

8 NOVEMBER
ON THIS DATE

On 8 November 1656 Edmond Halley was born. He's famous for working out the orbit of Halley's comet, and predicting its return. As well as his work in astronomy, he also designed diving bells, and dived beneath the surface of the River Thames in London in one of them.

9 NOVEMBER

One type of bacteria lives in caves where there's no light, and conditions are extremely acidic. Nothing else can live there. The bacteria hang from cave ceilings in slimy colonies, and scientists have called them snottites because they're like a cross between stalactites and snot!

10 NOVEMBER

If you find yourself wanting to talk to someone a very long way away, who can see you but can't hear you, the semaphore alphabet might come in handy. It's used by sailors at sea, and sometimes by beach lifeguards, or in mountainous areas. Most often people use flags, but you can also use paddles, lighted wands (useful at night), or just your hands.

6 NOVEMBER

'Pearl essence' gives a shimmery effect to lipstick. It's mostly made of herring fish scales!

7 NOVEMBER

A nineteenth-century cure for rheumatism (a disease that causes painful joints) was to carry a dead shrew in your pocket. It didn't work!

A/1   B/1   C/1

G/7   H/8   I/9

M   N   O

S   T   U

Y   T   REST/SPACE

11 NOVEMBER

The huge stones at Stonehenge in Wiltshire, England, were put there during the Bronze Age, and line up with the rising sun at the summer and winter solstices. All together, the stones at Stonehenge weigh about 1,850 tonnes – that's as much as 250 male African elephants!

12 NOVEMBER

Bats are the world's only flying mammals. There are more than 1,200 species, the biggest of which is the large flying fox, a type of fruit bat, with a wingspan of 1.8 metres. The smallest is the bumblebee bat, at just four centimetres long – and it's also the world's smallest mammal.

13 NOVEMBER

In Papua New Guinea, 820 different languages are spoken as a first language. The country's population is only about 3.5 million people!

14 NOVEMBER

In the 1600s, Antonie van Leeuwenhoek made his own microscopes and used them to record the first single-celled living things ever seen by human eyes. He found lots of them on the teeth of two old men who'd never brushed their teeth! Van Leeuwenhoek called the cells 'animacules' but today we call them bacteria.

15 NOVEMBER

Potatoes are safe to eat but the stems and leaves of the potato plant contain a poison called solanine. If a potato turns green, it might also contain the poison.

D/1   E/5   F/6

J/LETTERS   K/0   L

P   Q   R

V   W   X

NUMERALS   CANCELS   ERROR

16 NOVEMBER

The Aztecs and the Maya people of Central America both wrote in books made from bark. The Mayan writing system was the most complicated and used 700 different symbols. When the Spanish conquered Central and South America, they burned almost all the books.

17 NOVEMBER

The Sarawak Chamber in Malaysia is the biggest underground chamber in the world (as far as we know). It's so enormous that you could stand the Statue of Liberty inside it, with the Eiffel Tower laid across its width and One, World Trade Center laid along its length.

18 NOVEMBER

Famous nineteenth-century nurse Florence Nightingale had a pet owl, which she kept in her pocket. She'd rescued the owl from stone-throwing boys in Athens, and named it Athena.

19 NOVEMBER

Roughly nine out of a hundred people are colour blind, which means they have trouble telling the difference between some different colours. The condition is much more common in men than in women.

20 NOVEMBER

American swimmer Michael Phelps has more Olympic medals than anyone else – 28, gained in four Olympics. Of these medals, 23 are gold – another world record!

21 NOVEMBER

Jane Goodall spent 45 years studying wild chimpanzees in Tanzania. She was the first to observe and record them using tools, and because of her work people began to realise how similar chimps are to human beings. Her work is the longest continuous study of any animal in the wild.

22 NOVEMBER

Fossils of a human-like species called Homo floresiensis were discovered in 2003 on the island of Flores in Indonesia. These human-like creatures were only about a metre tall, with quite small brains, but hunted animals and used fire and stone tools. They died out around 12,000 years ago and they've been nicknamed Hobbits.

23 NOVEMBER

Tomatoes were introduced to Europe from South America in the sixteenth century. Many people believed they were poisonous and used tomatoes as decoration rather than food.

24 NOVEMBER
ON THIS DATE

On 24 November 1859, Charles Darwin's book *On the Origin of Species* was first published. As well as coming up with a theory about how all living things evolved, Darwin was fond of unusual food. At university Darwin was a member of the 'Glutton Club', where he ate unusual meat including hawks and owls. On his round-the-world voyage of discovery (where he came up with his evolutionary theory) he ate giant tortoises from the Galapagos islands, and was tucking into a tasty bird when he realised it was a rare species and sent the remains back to Britain to be identified.

25 NOVEMBER

A starfish can turn its stomach inside-out and push it out from its body to capture and eat its prey!

26 NOVEMBER

The British Empire grew to become the biggest empire of all time. Most of it was gained during the reign of Queen Victoria, but it reached its peak around 1920 when George V was king. It included India, Canada, Australia, New Zealand, bits of Africa, and more besides – about a quarter of the land and a quarter of the population of the world.

27 NOVEMBER

A compass points north, but not to the North Pole: the Earth's magnetic field doesn't quite line up with the North Pole, so there's a difference of about 25 kilometres.

28 NOVEMBER

Gary Dahl, who worked in the advertising industry in the US, came up with the idea of 'pet rocks' in the 1970s. You could buy a pet rock (just a rock in a box) for $4, including the 'training manual'. For some reason, the pet rocks became popular and made Dahl a millionaire.

29 NOVEMBER

Jupiter, the largest planet in our solar system, is very big indeed: it's 318 times the mass of Earth, and almost two and a half times the mass of all the planets in our solar system put together.

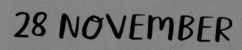

30 NOVEMBER

Blood makes up about 7% of your body's total weight. An adult's body contains about five litres of blood.

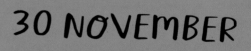

1 DECEMBER

The heaviest insects in the world are giant wetas, found in New Zealand. They look like enormous grasshoppers but they're too heavy to jump or fly. They weigh up to 70 grammes, and they can measure ten centimetres long with a leg span of 20 centimetres.

2 DECEMBER

Ancient Egyptians believed that when a person died, their heart would be weighed by the god Osiris. If it was heavier than the Feather of Truth, the Devourer ate it, and the person would not be able to enter the afterlife.

3 DECEMBER

Fruit flies were the first creatures sent into space. In 1957 Laika the dog became the first animal to orbit the Earth. Since then, lots of other animals have been rocketed into space including monkeys, apes, mice, tortoises, worms, butterflies, bees, spiders and jellyfish.

4 DECEMBER

Tutankhamun's tomb is the best-preserved Egyptian pharaoh's tomb ever discovered. It was found in 1922 by British archaeologist Howard Carter. Among the 5,000 treasures were a pair of the pharaoh's sandals, which had pictures of his enemies painted on the sole, so that he trod on them with every step!

5 DECEMBER

The Icelandic dish hakarl is made by leaving the meat of a Greenland shark to decay for several months, then hanging it up to dry for several more months. It smells strongly of ammonia and tastes very fishy. A lot of people find it absolutely disgusting! The meat of the shark is poisonous if it isn't treated in this way. Does that sound delicious or disgusting to you?

6 DECEMBER

In the seventh century, Empress Wuhou was the only woman ever to become Empress of China. She started off as a concubine (a sort of second-class wife) to the emperor, and managed to get the top job through a combination of cleverness, ruthlessness, and (probably) murder.

7 DECEMBER

Sound levels are measured in decibels. A sound too quiet to be heard by someone with normal hearing is set at 0 decibels. A decibel rating of 10 is ten times more powerful than the very quietest sound we're able to hear, 20 decibels is 100 times more powerful than the quietest sound, 30 decibels is 1,000 times more powerful, and so on. Here are some examples:

Rustling leaves: 10 decibels or less

An average snore: about 40 decibels

A classroom or office: about 50 decibels

A vacuum cleaner: about 80 decibels

8 DECEMBER

It's an unwritten rule amongst clowns that they shouldn't copy another clown's make-up. It sounds incredible, but circus clowns register the design of their make-up by decorating an egg, which is held in a central collection of clown egg faces. The tradition began in the UK in 1946, and has since spread to the US.

A car horn: 110 decibels

An extreme snore: about 110 decibels

A jet engine: 120 decibels

A gunshot: 140 decibels

9 DECEMBER

In 1974 Dr Henry Heimlich invented a way of dislodging food stuck in a person's airway, called the Heimlich manoeuvre. The manoeuvre has saved countless lives since then, but Dr Heimlich has only ever used his manoeuvre once: in 2016, at the age of 96, he saved a woman's life when she choked on a burger.

10 DECEMBER

The Sagrada Familia (Holy Family) cathedral in Barcelona was designed by the Spanish architect, Antonio Gaudí. Work on the cathedral started in 1883, and it's still not finished...!

11 DECEMBER

Oliver Cromwell got rid of King Charles I and ruled England himself, until he died in 1658. He was given a grand funeral and buried in Westminster Abbey. But two years later King Charles II was restored to the throne, and Cromwell was out of favour. His body was dug up, and his head was stuck on a pole in London, where it stayed for 24 years. The head passed from person to person for the next 300 years, at one point featuring in a freak show, until it was finally buried in 1960 in the grounds of Cromwell's old college in Cambridge.

12 DECEMBER

The coldest temperature ever recorded on earth was taken in Antarctica – minus 89.4°C. The world's hottest temperature was a blistering 70.7°C recorded in Iran in the Lut desert. Phew!

13 DECEMBER

In the early twentieth century, English eccentric W.Reginald Bray had the unusual habit of testing the postal system by posting unusual objects, including an unwrapped turnip with the address carved into it, onions, bicycle pumps, his dog, and himself. All arrived safely at their destinations.

14 DECEMBER
ON THIS DATE

On 14 December 1546, Danish nobleman Tycho Brahe was born. He became an astronomer who made careful and extremely useful observations of the stars, and he was also a brilliant mathematician. He was so passionate about maths that he fought a duel over a mathematical argument, and had his nose sliced off in the process! After that he wore a metal nose (and a golden one for special occasions).

15 DECEMBER

The amazing Amazon rainforest is home to an incredible variety of plants and animals. We are still discovering medical uses for some of the wildlife that grows there:

- 2.5 million different insect species
- At least 40,000 different plant species
- 3,000 different fish species
- 1,300 different bird species
- More than 400 different mammal species
- More than 400 different amphibian species
- Nearly 400 different reptile species

16 DECEMBER

The Atacama Desert in Chile is high above sea level, and the driest place on earth after Antarctica. In some parts of the desert rainfall has never been recorded!

17 DECEMBER
ON THIS DATE

On 17 December 1903 the Wright brothers – Wilbur and Orville – made the first ever sustained powered flight. The flight lasted 12 seconds and the plane travelled 36.5 metres.

18 DECEMBER

Gelada monkeys have the most complex communication sounds of all animals other than people, as far as we know. They live on high grasslands in Ethiopia and communicate with a wide variety of sounds and smack their lips. They sound uncannily like humans chatting to one another, and scientists think the monkeys might be a clue to how human beings evolved language.

19 DECEMBER

Sir George Sitwell was a wealthy aristocrat who spent his spare time creating unusual inventions, including a tiny pistol designed for shooting wasps!

20 DECEMBER

Most woolly mammoths died out around 10,000 years ago, but one small group survived on Wrangel Island in the Arctic until 1650 BC. The animals were well adapted to the icy conditions they lived in – they even had a special flap underneath their tails that protected their bottoms from the cold!

21 DECEMBER

The first zombie movie was *White Zombie*, made in 1932. Since then hundreds of zombie films have been made, including one called *The Incredibly Strange Creatures Who Stopped Living and Became Mixed-up Zombies*.

22 DECEMBER

Durians are a type of fruit from Southeast Asia that some people like to eat despite their foul smell, which is like raw sewage. It's so bad that durians have been banned on rail networks and at airports and hotels!

23 DECEMBER
ON THIS DATE

Two days before Christmas, the Mexican town of Oaxaca celebrates the Night of the Radishes to mark the introduction of radishes to Mexico. There's a big party with fireworks and – of course – a radish-carving competition, in which radishes are carved into all sorts of things: animals, people, buildings and nativity scenes.

24 DECEMBER

Mount Everest shrank by 2.5 centimetres after the 2015 earthquake in Nepal.

Welsh:
Nadolig Llawen

Afrikaans:
Geseënde Kersfees

Czech:
Veselé Vánoce

Turkish:
Mutlu Noeller

Danish:
Glaedelig Jul

Swahili:
Krismasi Njema

Dutch:
Vrolijk
Kerstfeest

Spanish:
Feliz Navidad

25
DECEMBER
CHRISTMAS DAY

How to say 'Happy Christmas' in 20 languages:

German:
Fröhliche
Weihnachten

Romanian:
Crăciun Fericit

Portuguese:
Feliz Natal

French:
Joyeux Noel

Norwegian
and Swedish:
God Jul

Finnish: Hyvää
Joulua

Macedonian:
Streken Boshik

German:
Fröhliche
Weihnachten

Italian:
Buon Natale

Greek: Kala
Christouyenna

Irish:
Nollaig Shona
Dhuit

Hawaiian:
Mele Kalikimaka

Hindi:
Subh Krisamas

26 DECEMBER

When satellites are no longer useful, sometimes they're returned to Earth – either they burn up in the atmosphere, or they crash-land somewhere remote, like the middle of the ocean. The 69-tonne satellite Skylab returned to Earth in 1979 and scattered huge chunks across the Australian desert, killing an unsuspecting cow.

27 DECEMBER

Baron Samedi has the job of leading the dead to the underworld in the Haitian voodoo religion. He has a skull face, wears dark glasses and a top hat, smokes a cigar, drinks rum, and tells rude jokes!

28 DECEMBER

Today, 6,912 different languages are spoken around the world. Only 239 of them originated in Europe. 94% of people speak 347 different languages. All the other 6,565 languages are spoken by just 6% of people.

29 DECEMBER

The mimic octopus can impersonate the appearance of other sea creatures, including jellyfish and sea snakes.

30 DECEMBER

A cat called Catmando was elected as the joint leader of the British political party, the Official Monster Raving Loony Party. The cat served as joint leader from 1999 to 2002 with his owner, Alan 'Howling Laud' Hope.

31 DECEMBER
NEW YEAR'S EVE

Some New Year's Eve traditions from around the world:

Denmark: stand on a chair and jump off it as midnight strikes.

DENM

PUERTO RICO

Puerto Rico: fill pots and pans with water and chuck it out of the house at midnight.

S

Spain: eat a grape for each strike of the clock at midnight.

TURKEY

Turkey: throw pomegranates out of windows on to the street below. The more mess, the more luck the coming year will bring.

CHILE

Chile: eat a spoonful of lentils at midnight for prosperity in the coming year.

Estonia: eat seven meals on New Year's Eve to give you strength for the year ahead.

ESTONIA